Leaving My Homeland

A Refugee's Journey from

Bhutan

Linda Barghoorn

CRABTREE
PUBLISHING COMPANY
WWW.CRABTREEBOOKS.COM

CRABTREE
PUBLISHING COMPANY
WWW.CRABTREEBOOKS.COM

Author: Linda Barghoorn

Editors: Sarah Eason, Harriet McGregor, Wendy Scavuzzo, and Janine Deschenes

Proofreader and indexer: Wendy Scavuzzo

Editorial director: Kathy Middleton

Design: Paul Myerscough and Jessica Moon

Cover design: Paul Myerscough and Jessica Moon

Photo research: Rachel Blount

Production coordinator and Prepress technician: Ken Wright

Print coordinator: Katherine Berti

Consultants: Hawa Sabriye and HaEun Kim, Centre for Refugee Studies, York University

Produced for Crabtree Publishing Company by Calcium Creative

Publisher's Note: The story presented in this book is a fictional account based on extensive research of real-life accounts by refugees, with the aim of reflecting the true experience of refugee children and their families.

Photo Credits:
t=Top, bl=Bottom Left, br=Bottom Right

Inside: Linda Barghoorn: pp. 7b, 10; Jessica Moon: pp. 5t, 12t; Shutterstock: Anandoart: p. 8; Atlaspix: p. 4t; Best-Backgrounds: pp. 22-23; Eagle9: p. 5; Fotosanka: p. 19t; Fritz16: pp. 11r, 13; Gnohz: pp. 8-9b; John Gomez: p. 29r; Great Vector Elements: p. 15tr; Jemastock: p. 20b; Kai19: p. 12; KiltedArab: p. 11b; Lawkeeper: p. 11t; Macrovector: p. 3; MC_Noppadol: p. 7t; MSSA: pp. 16b, 27tr, 28, 29t; Nakcrub: pp. 8-9t; Photoroyalty: p. 15tl; SAPhotog: pp. 20-21b; What's My Name: p. 21t; © UNHCR: pp. 14-15, 16; © UNHCR /Shikhar Bhattarai: p. 15b; © UNHCR/Jennifer Pagonis: pp. 18-19t; © UNHCR/John Rae: pp. 17, 18-19b, 26; © UNHCR/Peter de Ruiter: pp. 24, 25; © UNHCR/Kashish Das Shrestha: pp. 27t, 27b; © UNHCR/Deep Raj Uprety: pp. 20-21t; Wikimedia Commons: Alemaugil: p. 22.

Cover: Jessica Moon; Shutterstock: Lantaria (b).

Library and Archives Canada Cataloguing in Publication

Barghoorn, Linda, author
        A refugee's journey from Bhutan / Linda Barghoorn.

(Leaving my homeland)
Includes index.
Issued in print and electronic formats.
ISBN 978-0-7787-4684-3 (hardcover).--
ISBN 978-0-7787-4690-4 (softcover).--
ISBN 978-1-4271-2068-7 (HTML)

        1. Refugees--Bhutan--Juvenile literature. 2. Refugees--Nepal--Juvenile literature. 3. Refugee children--Bhutan--Juvenile literature. 4. Refugee children--Nepal--Juvenile literature. 5. Refugees--Social conditions--Juvenile literature. 6. Bhutan--Social conditions--Juvenile literature. I. Title.

HV640.5.B48B37 2018   j305.9'06914095498   C2017-907642-6
                                                     C2017-907643-4

Library of Congress Cataloging-in-Publication Data

Names: Barghoorn, Linda, author.
Title: A refugee's journey from Bhutan / Linda Barghoorn.
Description: New York : Crabtree Publishing, [2018] |
  Series: Leaving my homeland | Includes index.
Identifiers: LCCN 2017054805 (print) | LCCN 2017057135 (ebook) |
  ISBN 9781427120687 (Electronic HTML) |
  ISBN 9780778746843 (reinforced library binding : alk. paper) |
  ISBN 9780778746904 (pbk. : alk. paper)
Subjects: LCSH: Refugee children--Bhutan--Juvenile literature. |
  Refugees--Bhutan--Juvenile literature. | Bhutan--Emigration and immigration--Juvenile literature.
Classification: LCC HV640.5.B48 (ebook) | LCC HV640.5.B48 B37 2018
  (print) | DDC 305.9/06914095498--dc23
LC record available at https://lccn.loc.gov/2017054805

Crabtree Publishing Company
www.crabtreebooks.com   1-800-387-7650

Printed in the U.S.A./022018/CG20171220

Published in Canada
Crabtree Publishing
616 Welland Ave.
St. Catharines, Ontario
L2M 5V6

Published in the United States
Crabtree Publishing
PMB 59051
350 Fifth Avenue, 59th Floor
New York, New York 10118

Published in the United Kingdom
Crabtree Publishing
Maritime House
Basin Road North, Hove
BN41 1WR

Published in Australia
Crabtree Publishing
3 Charles Street
Coburg North
VIC, 3058

What Is in This Book?

Leaving Bhutan 4

My Homeland, Bhutan.. 6

Amita's Story: Life in Bhutan................................ 8

The Bhutan Conflict 10

Amita's Story: Leaving Bhutan............................ 12

Fleeing the Conflict 14

Amita's Story: Life in the Camp 16

Life in a Refugee Camp 18

Amita's Story: Moving On 20

Resettling the Refugees 22

Amita's Story: My Life in the United States 24

Challenges Refugees Face 26

You Can Help! 28

Glossary 30

Learning More.. 31

Index and About the Author................................ 32

Leaving Bhutan

In the early 1800s and 1900s, the tiny country of Bhutan needed workers and farmers to help build the country. Thousands of families from the nearby country of Nepal went to work there and raise families. At the time, Bhutan's government welcomed the Nepalese people. They settled in southern Bhutan. They were called Lhotshampas (lot-sham-puz), which means "people from the south."

The flag of Bhutan has an image of a dragon on it. The Bhutanese name for Bhutan is *Druk Yul (druhk yul)*. It means "Land of the Thunder Dragon."

China

Nepal

Bhutan

Bhutan is a small kingdom in Asia.

Bangladesh

India

Every child has rights. Rights are privileges and freedoms that are protected by law. **Refugees** have the right to special protection and help. The **United Nations (UN)** Convention on the Rights of the Child is a document that lists the rights that all children should have. Think about these rights as you read this book.

Some of the Lhotshampas have been living in refugee camps in Nepal for 20 years. Many children have been born in the camps.

By the 1970s, the Lhotshampas made up more than 25 percent of Bhutan's population. Because they practiced their own language and religion, the Bhutanese government was not happy. It saw them as a threat to the country's way of life, language, and religion. The government made laws that **discriminated** against the Lhotshampas. These laws **violated** their human rights.

The Lhotshampas protested against the government. They were arrested and put in jail, beaten, or killed. Thousands fled to live in refugee camps in Nepal. Refugees are people who flee their **homeland** because of war or other unsafe conditions. Refugees are different from **immigrants**. Immigrants choose to leave to look for better opportunities in another country.

My Homeland, Bhutan

Bhutan has many different landscapes. These range from untouched forests to snow-covered mountains and rich green valleys. The people of Bhutan have strong **traditions** rooted in their Buddhist religion.

Local leaders ruled small areas of the country until the 1600s. Then, a leader from the nearby country of Tibet united Bhutan as one country. Bhutan was then ruled by different kings for more than 100 years. Finally, in 2008, the fourth king turned the country into a **democracy**. Bhutan's citizens, or the people who lived there, then began to have a stronger voice in deciding their country's future.

Bhutan's Story in Numbers

The population of Bhutan is only

790,000.

The country is about the same size as Switzerland. But Switzerland has more than 10 times the number of people.

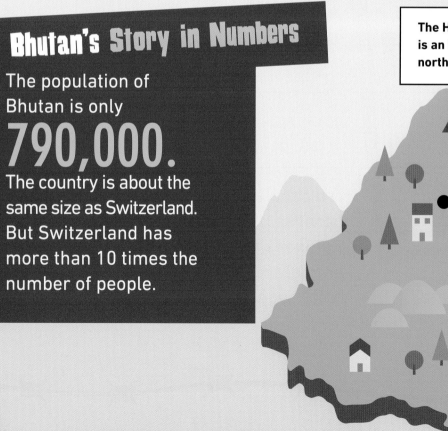

The Himalayan mountain range is an important part of Bhutan's northern landscape.

● Thimphu

Bhutan's capital city, Thimphu, is home to 150,000 people.

For many years, Bhutan's government kept the country cut off from the rest of the world. The government wanted to keep Bhutan's way of life and traditions the same. Up until 50 years ago, the country had no paved roads, cars, hospitals, or telephones. It was the last country on Earth to allow television. The Internet and television both arrived in 1999. They are still very restricted. Few foreigners are allowed to visit Bhutan.

To measure the country's success, the government created the idea of Gross National Happiness. The government measures the country's success in happiness rather than money. Some people have called Bhutan "paradise on Earth." But some of its **policies** have created hardships and violated peoples' rights.

Bhutan's landscapes are breathtaking and beautiful.

Amita's Story: Life in Bhutan

Our family had called Bhutan home for many years. My parents' grandparents came from Nepal. They came when Bhutan needed workers to help clear some of the forests for farmland and roads. The government was happy for the Nepalese workers to stay in Bhutan. They were allowed to own land. My parents worked very hard. They loved their farm in the village of Chapcha in southern Bhutan. They grew apples in their orchards and raised goats for milk and meat.

Many of the farmers in southern Bhutan can trace their roots back to Nepal.

I have never lived in Bhutan. I was born in a refugee camp in Nepal 11 years after my parents were forced to flee their homeland. What I know of Bhutan is from a few pictures and the stories my mother has shared. Sometimes, mother cries when she tells these stories. She cries when she talks about my grandparents. They stayed behind to take care of my parents' farm when my family left. I hope to meet them one day.

A typical Bhutanese house is made of mud, wood, and bamboo.

*My parents lived a peaceful life in Bhutan. Then new laws took away many of their rights. The school, which my eldest brother attended, was ordered to stop teaching in our Nepali language. The army often raided our village. Sometimes, they beat my parents and stole their food. They accused my parents of working against the government. My father attended a **demonstration** that protested against the army's actions. He was arrested and put in jail. After he was released, the police came to our home and threatened my parents. They were ordered to leave the country or risk being put in jail.*

Four out of five people live in Bhutan's countryside.

Bhutan's Story in Numbers

More than

2,000

Lhotshampas were beaten in Bhutan's prisons.

The Bhutan Conflict

In the 1980s, Bhutan's government created the "One Nation, One People" policy. This was meant to protect Bhutan's way of life, language, and religion. The new policy targeted the Lhotshampa people. The Lhotshampas had lived in Bhutan for many years. But they spoke their own language and followed their own traditions. They also practiced Hinduism, a religion different to that of the Buddhist Bhutanese.

The Lhotshampas were stripped of many of their rights. The government set limits on where they were allowed to go within the country. They could not hold government jobs or educate their children in the Nepali language. Many were forced to give up their land. When they spoke up for their rights, the government reacted harshly. Police raided homes, and arrested and beat people. Schools and health services were closed.

This is a statue of Buddha. He was a leader who started Buddhism. Approximately 75 percent of Bhutanese people follow the Buddhist religion.

New citizenship rules were also put in place. Immigrants who had been given citizenship in the 1950s were allowed to stay. But those who had come to Bhutan after that time were suddenly considered illegal, or not allowed by law. The government forced tens of thousands of people to leave. Many of them had been born and raised in Bhutan.

Refugee camps were built in Nepal for the people who were forced to leave Bhutan. The governments of Bhutan and Nepal refused to work together to find a solution to the problem. Many refugees spent years stuck in refugee camps in Nepal. They waited to be allowed to go home.

Some Lhotshampa refugees in Bhutan live in very poor conditions.

This building is one of the government offices in Bhutan. The Bhutanese government controls many aspects of life in Bhutan, including religion.

Amita's Story: Leaving Bhutan

Things happened quickly after the police threatened my parents. Several other families in the village had been arrested. They were not heard from again. Everyone was afraid of the police. My parents decided it was time to leave. They tried to convince my grandparents to come with them, but they refused. My grandparents said they were too old to start over in another country. They said they would stay in Bhutan and take care of the farm.

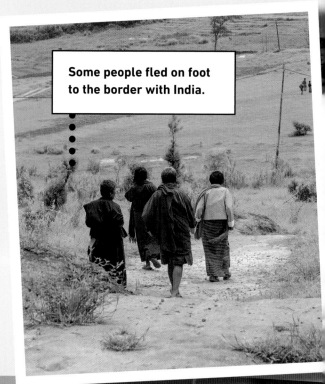

Some people fled on foot to the border with India.

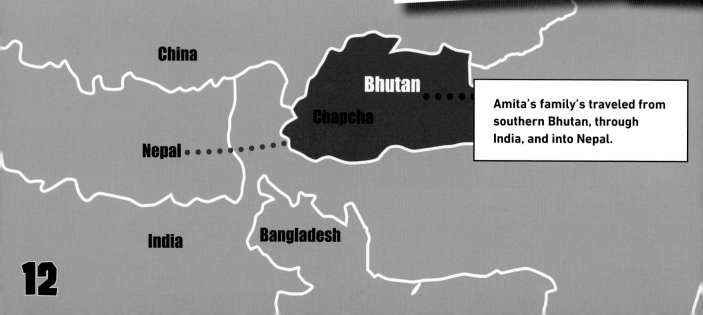

Amita's family's traveled from southern Bhutan, through India, and into Nepal.

China

Bhutan

Chapcha

Nepal

India

Bangladesh

Bhutan's Story in Numbers

More than

100,000

Lhotshampas fled Bhutan in the early 1990s to escape the government's threats.

Mother packed some clothes into two bags, and my family left the next morning. They boarded a truck that was headed for India. Other trucks carried people like my family, who were also trying to escape. When they arrived at the border with India, they were told that they were not welcome. There were buses that offered to take them to Nepal. They were promised a safe place to stay there. Tired and hungry, they climbed inside the buses with the other refugees.

Buses like this one were used to carry refugees to Nepal.

It was summer. The weather was hot and sticky. There was no food or water. Children's cries filled the bus. The bus journey to Nepal took four hours. The bus reached the refugee camp on the banks of a muddy river. Mother began to realize how serious the situation was. The camp was crowded, dirty, and disorganized. Many people were sick and dying. Mother held my older brother close as they were led to a tiny hut. It would become their new home.

Fleeing the Conflict

Many of the Lhotshampas owned land in southern Bhutan where they had settled. They raised cows and oxen, or grew crops. When they left Bhutan, most had to leave everything behind. Some Lhotshampas, such as Amita's grandparents, chose to stay in Bhutan. Families who were forced to separate had to make difficult decisions. Some never saw one another again.

Most of the refugees fled in trucks and made their way to the country's border with India. But India did not want to get involved in Bhutan's problems. The country worried about helping the refugees. India feared the Bhutanese government would take away the **hydroelectric power** it supplied them. So India put the refugees on buses again. It transported them to its border with Nepal, several hours away.

Some refugee camps set up lessons where refugees could learn to read and write English.

UN Rights of the Child

The government of the country where you live has a responsibility to protect your rights.

Nepal also did not want the refugees. But India made a deal with Nepal to move the refugees there. Nepal asked the **United Nations High Commissioner for Refugees (UNHCR)** for help, and they set up seven refugee camps. The camps ranged in size from 10,000 to 22,000 people. Most of the Lhotshampas who fled Bhutan ended up in one of these camps. A few were lucky enough to be allowed to settle in India or Nepal. They had family members they could join there.

Many refugee camps had only one water tap, like this one in a UNHCR refugee camp.

Amita's Story: Life in the Camp

My family stayed in a cramped, one-room bamboo hut. Mother spent hours each week waiting in long lines. She waited for the water to be turned on at one of the camp's wells. She also waited for one of the food baskets given out by the World Food Programme. She cooked outside over a small gas cooker. Mother worked hard to make good meals from the food **rations**. The cookers caught fire easily. Once a cooker caused a fire that destroyed more than 20 families' huts in the camp. Those families lost everything. They had to be moved until their huts could be rebuilt.

The refugee camps were overcrowded and dirty.

My aunt and four cousins arrived several months after my family. My uncle was not with them. He had been killed by police during a demonstration. My grandparents had not known our aunt would find my family in the camp. They could no longer get in touch with my grandparents. The only news they had of them came from people from their village who arrived at the refugee camp.

My family had been in the camp for 11 years when I was born. My parents now had four children. When I was two, my eldest brother Sonam became very sick. Mother had to take him to a doctor in a nearby village. They walked because they had no money for a bus. Sonam almost died before he was given the medicine that he needed.

Father often disappeared for days at a time. He left to do harvesting work nearby. Each time, Mother worried he would be arrested. Refugees were not allowed to work outside the camps. But we needed the money he made. We bought food, clothing, and soap when rations were not enough.

Huts made from bamboo were built very close together.

Life in a Refugee Camp

The refugees settled into simple, thatched bamboo huts. The camps were crowded and dirty. Daytime temperatures were extremely hot. Many people got sick and died from diseases.

Aid organizations arrived to provide food, water, health care, and education. But long lines at the health clinic were common. People with more complicated illnesses had to leave the camp to seek medical care. Food and water rations were the same for children and adults. This meant adults often did not get enough to eat. A family's typical food basket might contain rice, lentils, vegetable oil, salt, and some vegetables.

Refugees wait in long lines for food rations.

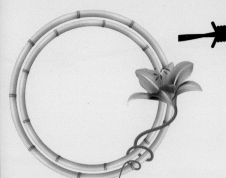

UN Rights of the Child

You have the right to special
protection and help as a refugee.

Some refugees tried to make money by working in the
camps' markets. They sold bamboo crafts. Others worked
illegally building roads or as field workers. The money
they earned helped support their families. Families were
desperate to make sure their children stayed in school.
They organized classes where high school students and
teachers volunteered. There was little to do in the camps
and people became bored or frustrated. Sometimes,
people used alcohol or drugs. **Human trafficking** was also
a problem. Girls were especially **vulnerable** in the camps.

One success story in these camps was the development of
the world's largest solar cooking project. This was funded
by a Dutch-Nepali organization
named the Vajra Foundation
Nepal. Solar cookers replaced
the gas-fueled cookers. They run
on the Sun's energy and reduce
the danger of accidental fires so
that families can cook safely.

**Solar cookers are used to
boil water and cook food.**

Amita's Story: Moving On

My family and I spent years waiting for news that we would be able to return to Bhutan. The governments of Bhutan and Nepal tried to find an agreement on what to do about the refugees. But they failed. We had little news from my grandparents. But we heard they had been forced by the government to give up the farm. My parents' hopes of ever being able to return home were fading.

When I was four years old, my parents decided to apply to the UNHCR resettlement program. They wanted to move to another country. They wanted my brothers and me to have a chance for a future. That included a good education and a safe place to live. Mother cried as they filled out the application forms. They completed the medical examinations, and attended interviews. She was afraid to stay in Nepal, but also afraid to leave.

This family has received good news. They will be resettled in the United States.

Every child has the right to live in freedom and dignity.

Finally, after more than 10 months, we were approved to go to the United States! Our papers giving us permission to leave Nepal were prepared. Travel arrangements were made for us. Late one afternoon, we boarded a bus to Nepal's capital city, Kathmandu. We spent several days there. We took English lessons and learned about what our new life would be like. They even taught us how to find our seats on the plane. We had never flown before.

When we arrived in the United States, we were met at the airport by a volunteer. She took us to a two-bedroom apartment with beds, flush toilets, and a refrigerator. She had to explain to us how to use these things and how to turn the lights on and off. Everything was new and exciting, but also scary.

Refugees travel by bus to Kathmandu to await resettlement.

Resettling the Refugees

Canada: 6,500

Years passed and the governments of Bhutan and Nepal refused to deal with the Lhotshampa refugees. Bhutan said that the refugees were not citizens, and should not be allowed to return. Nepal was busy fighting its own **civil war**. The government said it did not have enough money to help the refugees. Both countries wanted the refugees to be settled somewhere else.

United States: 84,819

Some refugees remain in refugee camps for many years.

United Kingdom: 358

Norway: 566

Denmark: 874

Netherlands: 327

By 2015, more than

100,000

Lhotshampa refugees had started new lives overseas.

New Zealand: 1,002

This map shows the numbers of refugees who resettled in North America, Europe, and Australia and Oceania.

Australia: 5,554

In 2007, the UNHCR began to organize a resettlement program. It was to relocate the refugees to new countries. Some refugees continued to hope that Bhutan might allow them to return one day. They worried about accepting an offer to another country. They might have to give up hope of returning to their beloved Bhutan.

The UNHCR's resettlement program was run between many organizations. These included aid groups, governments, and the **International Organization for Migration**. The program helped to resettle more than 80,000 refugees. It is one of the most successful programs of its kind. Today, only two camps remain in Nepal, with about 18,000 refugees. Many of them refuse to leave. They want to be allowed to return to Bhutan. Some want Nepal to give them land and allow them to live and work there.

Amita's Story: My Life in the United States

The first year of our new lives in Texas in the United States was challenging. We all had language lessons. My brothers and I found this much easier than my parents. They struggled to learn English. But it was important for us to learn how to support ourselves.

We had to find a doctor, and start school. We had to learn how to take a bus around the city. My father had to find a job. My mother learned how to shop for groceries. She wanted to cook our traditional foods. But my brothers and I wanted to try pizza and hot dogs.

The homes of refugees in their new countries are very different from their homes in Bhutan.

UN Rights of the Child

You have the right to an identity, which no one can take away from you.

My parents still dream of returning to Bhutan one day. We received news from my grandmother that my grandfather died last year. I am so sad that I never got to meet him. My aunt's family was able to join us here. Our families meet often to celebrate our festivals and religious holidays. There are other refugee families from Bhutan here, too. We all try to help each other.

Most people have been friendly to us and helped us feel welcome. My new friends at school want to know about my home country and what it was like. I do not know what to tell them. Where is my homeland? Is it Bhutan, where I have never lived? Is it Nepal, where I grew up in a refugee camp? The United States is my home now. But I hope to visit Bhutan one day to understand more about my homeland.

Refugee children go to new schools and learn English, math, and many other subjects.

Challenges Refugees Face

The Lhotshampa refugees were grateful for the chance to leave the refugee camps. But many of them found it difficult to accept that they might never see their homeland again. They did not want to travel to countries that were even farther away. They did not want to leave their homeland and family members. They worried about having to adapt to a culture that would be so different from their own.

Refugee families must adjust to cooking with and eating new foods.

Many refugees felt lonely. They were confused by the fast pace of life in the country they now called home. Most had never seen flush toilets, refrigerators, shopping malls, and homes with electricity. There were few rules to help them learn how to live outside a refugee camp. They would have to learn a new language. This would help them continue at school, find jobs, and feel part of the community.

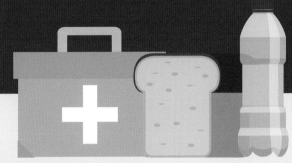

Adjusting to life in a new country can be both challenging and rewarding.

After settling in a new country, some refugees bring other family members over to live with them.

The Lhotshampas wanted to practice their culture and traditions in their new home. But they also had to learn the new culture of their **host country** and adapt to it. Sometimes, this meant accepting ideas that were different from theirs. Some refugees felt that they were not sure where in the world they really belonged. Sometimes, the city felt big and unfriendly. Sometimes, they came across **intolerance** and **racism** from people who were afraid of differences.

You Can Help!

There are many things you can do to help refugees and newcomers feel welcome in your community.

 Learn several simple greetings in the Nepali language. *Namaste (nah-mah-stay)* means "hello."

 Help refugees learn to shop for groceries or find their way around your neighborhood.

 Invite a newcomer at school to your home for dinner, or accept an invitation to their home.

 Volunteer at a local food bank or community center that supports newcomers.

 Collect clothing to support clothing drives, or collections, for newcomers or refugees.

 Do not judge a newcomer just because they look or act differently than you. Ask them to tell you about some of their customs and traditions.

UN Rights of the Child

Every child has the right to be protected from being hurt or mistreated.

AID

This protest march is showing people's support of refugees.

Discussion Prompts

1. Think about the Rights of the Child you have learned. Why are they important?
2. Why did the government of Bhutan discriminate against the Lhotshampas?
3. What are some of the challenges the refugees faced as they began life in a new country?

29

Glossary

civil war A war between groups of people in the same country

culture The way of life of a group of people, including their food, music, and other arts

democracy A form of government in which people vote for the leaders who represent them

demonstration An event where people gather to show their opinions on something

discriminated Treated someone unfairly or differently based on their gender, race, religion, or other identifiers

homeland The country where someone was born or grew up

host country A country that offers to give refugees a home

human trafficking The illegal movement of people

hydroelectric power Electricity produced by machines that are powered by moving water

immigrants People who leave one country to live in another

International Organization for Migration An organization made up of a group of governments that helps migrants

intolerance Unwillingness to accept different views or behaviors

policies Official sets of rules about what should be done

racism The belief that some races of people are not equal to others

rations A set amount of food and goods given to people regularly

refugees People who flee from their own country to another due to unsafe conditions

traditions Things that the people of a country have done for hundreds of years

United Nations (UN) An international organization that promotes peace between countries and helps refugees

United Nations High Commissioner for Refugees (UNHCR) A program that protects and supports refugees everywhere

violated Failed to respect

vulnerable At a great risk of being harmed

Learning More

Books

Bhutan Pocket Guide (Insight Pocket Guides). Insight Guides, 2017.

LeVerrier, Renee. *The Four Friends: A Bhutanese Folktale*.
Orchard House Press, 2012.

Tiwari, Hari. *The Story of a Pumpkin: A Traditional Tale from Bhutan*.
New Hampshire Humanities Council, 2013.

Websites

www.culturalorientation.net/learning/populations/bhutanese/video
Bhutanese refugees in the United States speak about their backgrounds
and their experiences as refugees.

www.ducksters.com/geography/country.php?country=Bhutan
This website contains lots of fascinating facts about Bhutan,
its history, geography, and people.

www.kingdomofbhutan.com/visitor/visitor_.html
Visit this site for detailed information about Bhutan and photographs of
festivals, landscapes, and people.

www.unicef.org/rightsite/files/uncrcchilldfriendlylanguage.pdf
Learn more about the United Nations Convention on the Rights
of the Child.

Index

Amita's story 8–9, 12–13, 16–17, 20–21, 24–25
arrests 5, 9, 10, 17

Buddhism 6, 10
buses 13, 14, 21

challenges 21, 24–25, 26–27
cookers 16, 19

English lessons 14, 21, 24, 25

farmers 4, 8, 12, 20

government 4, 5, 7, 8, 9, 10, 11, 13, 14, 20, 22

helping refugees 25, 28
history of Bhutan 4–5, 6–7, 8, 10–11
host countries 22–23, 24–25, 26–27

India 4, 12, 13, 14–15

landscapes 6, 7
Lhotshampas 4–5, 9, 10, 11, 13, 14–15, 22–23, 26–27

maps 4, 6–7, 12, 22–23

Nepal 4, 5, 8, 11, 12, 13, 14–15, 17, 19, 20–21, 22, 23

police 9, 10, 12, 17

rations 16, 17, 18
refugee camps 5, 8, 11, 13, 14–15, 16–17, 18–19, 22–23, 26
resettlement 20–21, 22–23, 24–25

sickness and disease 13, 17, 18

UN Rights of the Child 5, 11, 15, 19, 21, 25, 27, 29
UNHCR 15, 20, 23

About the Author

Linda Barghoorn studied languages in university because she wanted to travel the world. She has visited 56 countries, taking photographs and learning about different people and cultures. Her father traveled to North America as a German immigrant more than 50 years ago. Linda has written 14 children's books and is writing a novel about her father's life.